The Neutral Eye

The Neutral Eye

SEEING PAST THE LABELS OF FEAR, GREED & GOD

SURAAJ PARAB

Foreword by Sandeep Thakur

For permissions, inquiries, or media requests, contact:
bassuraaj@gmail.com

ISBN:
Paperback: 978-93-5812-419-4
Hardcover: 978-93-5813-885-6

First edition published: 2026

Cover design, Interior layout by Suraaj Parab

This is a work of nonfiction. Names, locations, and conversations have been reproduced from memory and, in some cases, altered or reimagined for privacy, narrative clarity and emotional truth.

For my Mama,

who taught me that truth is not a gift—
it is an observation.
You showed me how to stand on the earth
and trust my own gaze.
This work is the residue of your vision.

SANTOSH SHELAR
1966 – 2022

The body follows the mind;
The mind follows the thoughts;
The thoughts follow the Belief.

Shift the Belief, and the system aligns.

— Suraaj Parab

Foreword

by Sandeep Thakur

Some books are read. Some are understood. Then there are those rare ones that feel like they were written through you.

The Neutral Eye is that kind of book for me.

I have known Suraaj Parab for over fifteen years. I know him not just as a musician, but as a human being in constant evolution. We have shared stages, music, silences, and the many unpredictable turns of life. I've seen him at his physical peak and at his most vulnerable.

I have watched him rebuild himself—not once, but repeatedly—with a discipline and honesty that is rare.

Suraaj is a pianist, a composer, a bassist. But beyond those labels, he is a seeker. Perhaps that is what these pages truly represent.

Many describe him as an atheist. I see it differently. Suraaj isn't rejecting belief; he is questioning borrowed belief. There is a depth in his thinking that defies definitions, and that depth is what you are about to experience.

His journey has been anything but easy. From battling physical limitations to enduring the profound loss of his mother, Suraaj has walked through fires that test the very core of a soul.

What stands out isn't the struggle. It is the clarity he carved out of the wreckage.

The Neutral Eye doesn't offer the comfort of easy answers. It does something far more valuable: it invites you to look at your life without distortion. No labels. No inherited narratives.

As I read, I often felt like I was hearing my own thoughts articulated with a precision and courage I deeply admire. It resonated with me intellectually, emotionally, and spiritually.

Suraaj's first book, **Her,** gave us a glimpse into his inner world. With **The Neutral Eye,** he takes it further. He is stripping away layers, challenging perceptions, and urging you to confront your own truths.

This is a no-nonsense body of work. It is dignified, sharp, and unapologetically honest.

If you have ever questioned your beliefs, your identity, or the noise around you—this book will speak to you.

I don't recommend this lightly. I recommend it because I have lived

parts of it alongside the man who wrote it.
Suraaj Parab does not just write these words. He lives them.

- Sandeep Thakur

Table of Contents

THE NEUTRAL EYE

Prologue

The Weight of The Gold

I sat in a room filled with 23 symbols of my own excellence. The world called them "Awards." My ego called them "Armor." To the industry, they were proof of my "Greatness." To my family, they were proof of my "Success." But through the **Clinical Eye** (Chapter 6), they were just heavy objects reflecting light—gold-plated mass taking up physical space in a room.

I had spent seven years chasing these labels, running on a high-speed treadmill of "Greed" (Chapter 4), believing that once I had accumulated enough of them, the internal **"Muffling"** would stop. I thought if I was "Great" enough, I would finally be "Free." I thought if the world clapped loud enough, I would finally be able to hear my own voice.

But the opposite happened. The louder the applause, the more the "Original Code" (Chapter 5) was drowned out. I wasn't becoming a "Source"; I was becoming a **Collection of Definitions.** I was "Suraaj Parab: The Award-Winning Musician." I was "Suraaj Parab: The Successful Son." But I was no longer Suraaj Parab: The Being.

I saw the same pattern everywhere I looked. I saw people fighting over their egos, defending "Labels" like they were defending their own children. I saw them ruled by the **Pulse of Fear** (Chapter 3) and the **Hunger of Greed** (Chapter 4), completely forgetting who they were before the world told them who they should be.

We are born with a **Natural Calling**—a unique, exceptional potential that doesn't require a script or a scripture. But the moment we enter the world, the "Labeling" begins.

- It starts in the kitchen, where a child's joy is labeled as "Noise."
- It continues in the school, where curiosity is labeled as "Distraction."
- It solidifies in the temple and the office, where obedience is labeled as "Goodness."

By the time we are adults, we are walking "Handicaps" (Chapter 5). We are so covered in the "Social Dust" of other people's expectations that we can no longer feel the wind on our skin. We waste our lives in a **"Temporal Stutter,"** chasing a future "Success" that is just another label to add to the cage.

I wrote this book because I reached the end of the labels and found nothing there. I realized that the "God-Bias" (Chapter 5) and the "Tribe-Fear" (Chapter 3) were just ghost stories designed to keep the "Herd" (Chapter 9) from ever looking at the world directly.

I tried to dissect how these labels get pulled on us, like a skin we never asked for. I wanted to show you that seeing the world in a **Neutral Way** is not "Coldness"—it is **Clarity.** When you stop labeling a tragedy as "Bad" or a trophy as "Good," your life becomes calm. It becomes beautiful. Paradoxically, it even becomes more successful, because you are no longer wasting energy fighting the "Descriptions" of the world and can finally start interacting with the **World itself.**

This is not a "Self-Help" book. I am not here to give you new, "Better" labels to wear. I am not here to tell you how to be a "Happier Person" or a "More Productive Worker." Those are just more cages.

I am here to help you **Deconstruct**. I am here to help you apply the "Clinical Eye" to your own armor until you see it for what it is: weight. We are going to walk through the "God-Bias," the "Geopolitical Herd," and the "Mirror of Love" until the only thing left is the **Residue** (Chapter 8)—the quiet, undeniable alignment of a soul that has finally stopped trying to be "Something" and has started being **Everything**.

If you are tired of the "Muffling," if you are tired of the "Temporal Stutter," and if you are ready to see the "World Restored" (Chapter 10), then let us begin.

My name is **Suraaj Parab**, and this is my perspective of looking at the world.

" The door to the cage was never locked.
You just needed to stop labeling it as "Home."

Part I
The Architecture of the Filter

Chapter 1:
The Inherited Lens

Before your heart ever learned to pulse against the constraints of a ribcage, there was a silence. It wasn't the hollow silence of a lonely room; it was a vast, heavy quiet. A belonging. In that space, you weren't a "person" with a name to defend or a face to fix in a mirror. You had no language to trap your thoughts, no bitter memories to ache over. You simply were.

You existed as a presence in something boundless, untouched by the frantic itch of desire or the cold shiver of fear. Some say we once saw Truth without the smudge of human fingerprints on it. Others feel it as a vibrating echo—the way you can smell the salt of an ocean long before you see the waves.

Then, the gravity sets in. The soul begins to narrow. It condenses, preparing for the heavy burden of bone and the suffocating beauty of time. By the time you arrived, you had forgotten the vastness. But sometimes, in the dead of night or the pause between breaths, you feel the ghost of it. You feel like you belong to something more.

A child enters the world without categories. To a child, the world isn't a map of "safe" and "dangerous"—it is a symphony of sensations. A color isn't a warning; a sound isn't a judgment. Everything arrives raw, unfiltered, like white light shattering through a prism for the very first time.

The body understands before the mind can ever speak. The child reaches out because something inside them **moves**—a curiosity that asks no permission.

Then comes the "Ordinary Day."

Imagine a child sitting on a sun-drenched rug. The air is thick with the smell of dust and safety. Suddenly—a crash. A heavy glass vase shatters nearby. The child's body reacts first: a sharp jolt, eyes wide, a frantic drum of the heart against the ribs.

This isn't fear. Not yet. It is intensity. The nervous system is waking up, trying to digest this electric new sensation of "Loud." The child looks at the shards, mesmerized by the way they steal the light.

Then, a voice slices through the air. Sharp. Certain.

"No! That's bad! Don't touch that!"

The child doesn't argue. They can't. To a child, a parent's voice isn't just an opinion—it is the architecture of reality. But inside the body, a silent war is born. The sensation felt alive, even exciting. But the label said: **Bad.** In that moment, the child learns to fear their own curiosity.

Before the child learns the word "Bad," they learn the weight of Shame. Watch a toddler discover a mud puddle. To them, that mud is a miracle. It is cool, viscous, transformative. They press their palms into it, feeling the earth squeeze between their fingers. There is no "dirty" in their vocabulary—only "texture." They are engaging with the world in its most honest form.

But then, the adult arrives. There is a gasp. A frantic reaching for wet wipes. A face twisted in disgust. "Look at you! You're a mess! That's gross!"

In that moment, the child's internal compass spins wildly. Their skin felt cool and connected to the earth, but the authority says that feeling is a transgression. This is the first coat of paint on the soul's window. The child learns that their simple joy—the tactile truth of their existence—is a source of disappointment for the people they need for survival.

Slowly, the child stops touching. They start checking. They look at their hands not to see what they can create, but to see if they are "clean" enough to be loved.

We must ask: where did the "Bad" come from?

When a parent reacts with a sharpness that seems too heavy for the moment, they aren't reacting to you. They are reacting to a shadow standing behind them.

My mother was a person of immense love. Everything I am—the breath in my lungs and the path I walk—is a testament to her hard work and sacrifice. But she was a carrier. She was raised in a house where my grandfather's arrival was signaled by a terrifying silence. When his boots hit the floor, the air died. Everything went quiet because noise was a risk.

She was a brilliant student, scoring 90% or higher, but in that house, a 90% was just a 10% failure. She was scolded for the sliver of space between her and the topper. That pressure doesn't just disappear when you grow up; it hardens. It turned her inward. It taught her that feelings are dangerous things that must be swallowed until they ferment and eventually explode as anger.

By the time I arrived, the baggage was packed and ready to be handed down.

She replicated the only architecture of "safety" she knew: strictness, anger, the demand for a perfection that doesn't exist in nature. As a child, I didn't see a woman struggling with her past; I saw a wall. I became a ghost in my own home, an introvert who weighed every thought before speaking, terrified of the verdict. I wasn't living my life; I was navigating her trauma.

Later in life, she had the grace to look back and see the wreckage. She admitted she was wrong. She saw the ghost. But by then, the "Inherited Lens" was already over my eyes. She didn't mean to infect me; she was simply breathing the only air she had ever known. We think we are being "disciplined," but often, we are just being trained to carry the weight our parents were too tired to hold anymore. We pass on our fears like a virus, disguised as "wisdom."

This brings me back to that video—the one that haunted my sleep.

A toddler, no more than three years old, was sitting calmly among three massive pythons—fifteen feet of raw muscle and scales. To any adult, this is a nightmare. Our skin crawls; our heart rate spikes. We see "predator." We see "death."

But the child? The child was stroking the snake's cold skin as if it were the soft fur of a puppy. There was no flinch. No hesitation. To that child, the snake was simply another "Is." It was a movement, a texture, a presence.

At 32 years old, I watched that screen with a knot of anxiety in my stomach, waiting for the tragedy. But the tragedy had already happened to me, decades ago. The child was interacting with life; I was interacting with a label.

Almost 90% of humans share this bone-deep fear of snakes. We think it's "natural." But that child proves it isn't. We aren't born with tags that say **Fear This or Love That**. Those tags are pinned onto us.

When we do something that defies a social norm, we are punished—physically, or through the coldness of a parent's withdrawal. That action installs the label. The label becomes the wall. We don't see the snake; we see the "Bad" we were told was there.

This is how the lens is inherited. It isn't a violent takeover; it's a slow, subtle dusting. It is a thousand small moments where the world stands between you and your experience.

- **"This is good."**
- **"That is ugly."**
- **"This is how a boy acts."**
- **"That is wrong for a girl to feel."**

Each word settles over your raw experience like dust on a mirror. Slowly, the reflection grows dim. You stop trusting the jolt in your chest and start looking at the faces around you to see how you should feel. You become an expert at reading others and a stranger to yourself.

We are living in Plato's Cave, watching shadows on the wall and calling them "Real," never realizing the light is behind us. Even our identity—our very names—is an inheritance we didn't ask for. We are carrying patterns encoded in DNA and reinforced by the ghosts of our ancestors' fears.

The child does not realize what is being lost because nothing is taken away suddenly. It is replaced.

Experience is replaced with Interpretation.

Curiosity is replaced with Instruction.

Feeling is replaced with Meaning.

And slowly, almost beautifully, the child learns how to see the world... not as it is... but as it has been told to be. They become a "success" in the eyes of the world, but a hollow echo in their own heart.

But somewhere, very deep beneath the layers of "Right" and "Wrong," the first experience never truly disappears.

The rawness of that sound. The quiet pull toward that color. The lack of fear for the snake. They remain untouched, like ancient cave paintings hidden behind a modern wall. They are the "Natural Calling."

They are suppressed by the pressure of the family, the school, the church, and the screen. They are buried under the weight of being a "Good Person." But they are not dead.

Because before the world was explained to you... before anything was called good or bad... you did not see through a lens. You simply saw.

And the work of your life—the true philosophy—is not to learn more labels, but to start peeling them off until you can see that way again.

"We are born with eyes,
but we are raised with filters.
The first tragedy of a life is learning to name a thing
before you have actually seen it."

Chapter 2: The Gravity of Certainty

There is a force within the human mind that does not announce itself, yet it governs more than we realize. It is not truth. It is not even knowledge.

It is the primitive, addictive **feeling of being right.**

Long before a thought becomes a belief, and long after evidence begins to fracture it, there exists a quiet attachment—a tightening around an idea that says: This is how things are. Not because it has been tested, but because it has been repeated until it feels like skin.

Certainty is not born from clarity. It is born from familiarity.

The brain does not seek truth in the way we imagine; it seeks **stability.** Within its neural pathways, patterns are rewarded not for being accurate, but for being consistent. Every time a belief is reinforced, a subtle hit of dopamine follows—a release, a settling, a momentary quieting of the world's chaos.

To be right is not just to understand. **To be right is to feel safe.**

And so, when a contradiction appears, it does not arrive as a neutral event. It arrives as an intruder. Something tightens in the solar plexus before the mind can even find the words to argue. The breath hitches. The jaw sets. There is a rise in tension, almost imperceptible, but unmistakably hostile. Because to encounter something that should not exist within your framework is not just to face new information—it is to face a tremor in the ground you stand on.

Why is this tremor so terrifying? Because from our very first breath in the "tribe," we are taught that to be "wrong" is to be cast out.

Think back to the elementary school playground. It's Sports Day. The sun is hot, the air smells of cut grass and nervous sweat. You are standing at the starting line of a race. The whistle blows.

Society has a very specific "Science of the Win." We are biologically wired to seek status because, for our ancestors, status meant survival. The winner of that race doesn't just get a plastic gold medal; they get the **Roar**. They get the smiles of the teachers, the pride of the parents, the invisible "Yes" from the universe.

But look at the child who finishes last.

Watch their face. They aren't just tired; they are humiliated. There is a deafening silence when they cross the line. No one claps for the struggle of the slow. This creates a neural blueprint: To win is to be loved. To lose is to be invisible. By the time we are adults, this "Win/Loss" binary has infected our very perception of reality. We stop looking for the truth and start looking for the "Win." We would rather defend a lie that keeps us in the "Winner's Circle" of our social group than admit a truth that makes us look "wrong" or "slow" in front of the tribe. We are addicted to the applause of being right, even if we are being right about a life that is making us miserable.

We often talk about "truth" as if it's a destination we are all trying to reach. But in reality, most of us are running away from it.

In the film The Matrix, there is a moment that has become a modern myth. Morpheus offers the hero, Neo, a choice. Two pills. One blue, one red.

The **Blue Pill** is the return to the comfortable illusion. The **Red Pill** is the descent into the harsh, cold reality. I believe every person in this world already knows the solution to their deepest problems. We aren't looking for answers; we are looking for an escape from the discomfort of the answer. Most of us choose the Blue Pill. We decide to live comfortably in a lie rather than suffer in the truth.

For 21 years of my life, I lived in the Blue Pill. I was morbidly obese. I weighed **146kg**, my waist stretching to **42 inches**.

Every morning I woke up in a body that was a physical manifestation of my refusal to see the truth. People think the "truth" for an obese person is a secret diet or a magic pill. It's not. Every person struggling with their weight knows the formula: stop overeating, eat clean, move the body, address the underlying rot.

But accepting that truth is the Red Pill. And the Red Pill tastes like iron.

When I finally decided I didn't want to live that lie anymore, my life became uncomfortable as hell. For years, I was in a cage match with my own biology. I would pull my hair out in frustration, the animal inside me screaming to eat, while the soul inside me whispered to stop. I had to stop choosing the lie of "I'm fine" to embrace the agony of "I am changing."

But we must be honest: the world is designed to make the Red Pill as hard to swallow as possible. We live in a **Comfort Trap**.

Everywhere you look, there is a "Blue Pill" being sold to you. It's in the infinite scroll of your phone that numbs the anxiety of your own thoughts. It's in the "highly palatable" processed food that spikes your dopamine so you don't have to feel your own emptiness. It's in the entertainment that allows you to live vicariously through others because your own life feels too heavy to carry.

The Comfort Trap is a billion-dollar industry. It is the anesthetic of the modern soul.

If you feel that "internal friction"—the restlessness that tells you something is wrong—the world tells you to fix it with a purchase, a pill, or a distraction. It tells you that discomfort is a "glitch" to be deleted. But that discomfort isn't a glitch. It is your soul's last attempt to wake you up. It is the friction of the Red Pill trying to break through.

When you choose comfort over truth, you aren't just relaxing; you are sedating the only part of you that can actually change your life. You are choosing a slow, cushioned death over a sharp, painful awakening.

The mind resists this awakening instinctively. It doesn't always scream "No!" Sometimes it uses quieter, more sinister tools: reinterpretation, dismissal, distortion.

We don't always reject the evidence directly. Instead, we bend it. We reshape the facts just enough so they can fit into the rusted cage of what we already believe. We do this because accepting the truth fully would require something far more violent than "updating a thought."

It would require **undoing.**

And undoing is not a cognitive act. It is a physical one. It feels like tearing a muscle. There is a friction that emerges when reality and belief refuse to align. One part of the mind sees the truth; another part refuses to let go of the lie. This is the gravity of certainty—a pull so strong it bends the very light of perception until the line between what is happening and what we think is happening disappears.

Yet, beneath this rigid fortress of "Winning" and "Being Right," something quieter survives.

There is a faint, overlooked space in the mind that can still observe without judging. A space where the experience hasn't been named yet, hasn't been forced to "behave."

To step into that space requires a different kind of strength. Not the strength to defend what you know, but the **willingness to stand naked without it**. To feel the tension of being "wrong" and not rush to resolve it. To see the world without needing to be right about it.

Because beyond the gravity of certainty—beyond the walls we build to feel safe—there is something far less stable, but far more real.

"Certainty is not a strength; it is a weight.
We anchor ourselves to a single 'Truth'
because we are terrified of the tide,
forgetting that a heart made of stone can only sink."

Part II
The Three Great Distortions

Chapter 3: The Pulse of Fear

Before a belief becomes a cage... before a boundary is drawn and defended with a snarl... there is something far more primitive at work.

Fear.

Not the loud, cinematic fear that arrives in moments of visible danger. I'm talking about the quiet, constant pulse. The kind that hums in the background of your life like a refrigerator you've stopped noticing until the room goes silent. Fear does not ask for your permission, and it certainly doesn't wait for clarity. It marks you first—and explains itself later.

In the beginning, it's just a sensation. A slight, nagging hitch in the center of your chest. A shortening of breath that never quite reaches the basement of your belly. You feel a subtle contraction, a bracing in the shoulders, as if your body is preparing for a blow that never lands. There is no visible threat. No immediate harm. And yet, the body behaves as if something is always about to happen.

Over time, this sensation begins to organize itself. It searches for objects, for explanations, for somewhere to attach its presence. Because a feeling without a reason is a ghost you can't fight; but a feeling with a label becomes manageable.

So, the mind provides one: Outside is unsafe. Change is risky. Movement is dangerous.

The world is divided quietly, not through direct experience, but through the primal need to contain this constant tension. And so, a space is created. Not visibly, not physically at first... but undeniably real. A boundary. Inside, there is familiarity. Predictability. Control. Outside, there is uncertainty. The unknown. Exposure.

We like to think of ourselves as logical beings, navigating life through a series of calculated risks. We aren't. We are simpler than that. Almost every decision we make—who we talk to, where we go, what we dare to dream—is a reaction to a software installed in us before we could even walk.

It starts with a skinned knee and a voice from above.

Think back to the first time you tried to run. You were small, the world was vast, and your legs were shaky but eager. You fell. The pavement was cold and unforgiving. In that moment, you weren't "afraid"; you were just hurt. There is a vital difference. Pain is a physical fact, but fear is an interpretation.

Then came the voice of love—sharp, panicked, and heavy with the weight of "I told you so."

"I told you not to run! Look what happened. See? This is what happens when you don't listen."

In that second, the lesson wasn't "be careful." The lesson was **"the world is a trap."** Our parents, in their desperate need to keep us breathing, accidentally teach us to stop living. They wrap us in the bubble wrap of their own anxieties. They don't say, "You will fall when you try to run, but don't be afraid of the ground." They say, "Don't run, because the ground is waiting to break you." This overprotectiveness is a slow-acting toxin. It installs a software of hesitation that runs in the background for the next thirty years. We begin to label the impulse to explore as "Bad" and the impulse to hide as "Good." We mistake our parents' limitations for the laws of the universe.

We become so rooted in this inherited fear that we find ourselves paralyzed in a hilarious, tragic contradiction: W**e are terrified of death because we won't be alive... yet we are terrified to live because we might die.**

We treat life like a glass vase we're afraid to drop, so we keep it tucked away in a dark cupboard. We don't realize that a vase in a cupboard is just a piece of clay—it only fulfills its purpose when it's out in the light, holding water, risking the breeze.

We spend our days calculating the "wrong" moves.

"If I quit this job, I might starve."

"If I say how I feel, they might leave."

"If I step out, I might fall."

We stay in the loop, vibrating with the "pulse" of what might happen, until the clock runs out. We find our "solution" only when the breath finally leaves us, realizing too late that the door to the cage was never actually locked.

The truth is, we suffer maximum in our imagination and very little in reality. Reality is a single blow; imagination is a thousand cuts.

Reality is the fall; fear is the endless, gut-wrenching drop that happens in your mind every night before you go to sleep. We are being haunted by ghosts we've invited into our own living rooms.

I saw this most clearly in my father. I remember when mobile phones first arrived. They weren't tools then; they were alien artifacts. Because the human mind is wired to label what it doesn't understand as "dangerous," the myths spread like a virus.

The whispers were everywhere: The RF waves cause cancer. The radiation will rot your brain. These things are killers.

My father was paralyzed by these stories. He avoided buying one for a long time, looking at those early devices as if they were grenades with the pins pulled out. He was feeling the weight of a cancer that didn't exist, fighting a battle against waves he couldn't see, mourning a health he hadn't even lost.

Then, the day came. He bought one.

The box was opened. He held it to his ear. **Nothing happened.** The sky didn't fall. His brain didn't melt. The fear that had felt as solid as a stone wall for months simply evaporated into the air. It wasn't that the world became safe; it was that the imagination finally ran out of lies to tell.

Now, we can't imagine a minute without these devices. The "monster" of the past is the lifeline of today. This is the trick fear plays: it presents a "what if" as a "will be." It forces you to pay interest on a debt you might never owe.

The cage doesn't just dictate where we go; it dictates what we find "revolting." For my entire life, that boundary was insects. If a cricket landed near me, my skin would crawl. It was a reflex—a primitive, frantic need to kill it or erase it from my sight.

Then, I found myself in a night market in Thailand.

The air was thick with lemongrass and hot oil. There they were, piled high: **Crispy bamboo worms. Creamy silkworm pupae. Crunchy grasshoppers**. The old program in my head screamed Bad! Dirty! Dangerous! But a new thought pierced through: "A healthy human, just like me, eats these every day. It is part of their truth. If it were disgusting, they wouldn't be smiling." The only thing making it "bad" was the label I brought with me.

I reached out. I took a grasshopper. I bit down. Crunch.

It wasn't a horror movie. It was savory, salty, and rich. Within minutes, the "monsters" were becoming a feast. I wasn't just eating protein; I was eating my fear. I was realizing that the thing I feared had no power over me once I stopped labeling it.

When I told my mother later, her face was a map of horror. She looked at me as if I'd swallowed glass. In her eyes, I had done something "gross." But looking at her, I realized I was finally the one who was free. She was still living in the world where insects were "Bad." I was living in a world where they were just dinner.

Stagnation does not feel like decay when it happens slowly. It feels like "normal."

Each day that passes without stepping beyond the boundary becomes evidence that the boundary is necessary. The absence of immediate danger is not seen as neutrality... but as validation. Nothing bad happened today because nothing was risked.

And so, the cage strengthens. Not through bars, but through repetition. Fear no longer feels like a reaction; it feels like the Truth.

There are moments, however—brief and almost imperceptible—where something shifts. A quiet awareness that the boundary may not be as absolute as it seems. In those moments, the body reacts before the mind can explore it. The breath tightens further. The chest constricts.

Because the cage is not just built around the body. It is built within it. To leave it is not simply to move outward. It is to confront the very sensation that created it. To allow the breath to deepen when it has learned to stay shallow. To stand in a space where certainty does not protect, and familiarity does not contain.

Fear resists this. It pulls back. It contracts. It reminds: Stay here. This is safe. Even when safety begins to resemble stillness... and stillness begins to resemble absence.

Don't be fearful of falling. You will fall when you try to run. But if you never run, you are already dead—you just haven't stopped breathing yet. Fear doesn't just warn you against danger; it defines the limits of life itself. Break the label, and the bars vanish.

"Fear is a vibration of the mind
that we mistake for the architecture of the world.
Stop trying to kill the monster
and start observing the pulse;
the shadow only grows
when you turn your back to the light."

Chapter 4:
The Hunger of Greed

We are driven by two primal engines: **Fear and Greed.** In our world of labels, we often cast Fear as the villain and Greed as the "ambition" that builds civilizations. But strip away the moralizing, and you'll find they are merely two sides of the same heavy coin—the coin of **Attachment**. Fear is the greed for safety; it is the desperate, clutching desire to keep things exactly as they are. But Greed? Greed is the fear of arrival. It is the terror that if we stop reaching, we will cease to exist.

We trade our wings for a sturdy cage and call it a "good deal," never realizing that the cage is empty because we aren't even truly inside it. We are already halfway down the road, chasing a shadow of who we think we should become.

Two thousand years ago, the Roman philosopher **Seneca** looked at the bustling streets of Rome—a city obsessed with conquest, gold, and legacy—and saw the same sickness we carry today. He wrote to his friend Lucilius about a specific kind of madness: strenua inertia. It translates to "restless idleness" or "busy doing nothing." It describes the man who is always in a hurry, always "getting ahead," but who never actually goes anywhere because his soul is not present for the journey.

Seneca observed the Roman elite—men who conquered provinces but could not sit still in a quiet room. He realized that a man who has little but wants nothing more is truly wealthy, while the man who has a palace but is already sketching the blueprints for his next villa is a beggar.

Greed is not the desire to have. It is the inability to **arrive.**

When we are possessed by this hunger, our senses begin to dull from underuse. We become like those Romans at their banquets, chewing on peacock tongues and honeyed wine while their minds were already at the next political appointment. They chewed, but they did not taste. They won, but they did not feel. They were "displaced." They were ghosts in their own triumphs.

I see my own face in Seneca's mirror. For Seven years, I was a citizen of that restless Rome. I was a man possessed by the "Next."

In that span, I won twenty-three prestigious international awards. I became a voting member of the Grammys. I birthed over forty songs.

On paper, I was an emperor. I was ascending the marble steps of my industry, and with every trophy, I thought I was buying another brick of "Security." I thought that if I could just stack enough gold on the shelf, the "Pulse of Fear" from Chapter 3 would finally stop.

But the "Hunger of Greed" is a master of disguise. It told me I was working for my family. It told me I was writing music to find a "muse"—to find someone to love with my whole heart. I was chasing the idea of love, projecting it onto future melodies and distant horizons. I was treating my life like a draft, thinking the "final version" would start once I reached the summit.

This is what the Stoics called the "Leaning Soul." Greed creates a temporal stutter—a refusal to let the foot land fully on the ground because the eyes are already scouting the next step. We treat the current moment like a disposable wrapper that must be torn away to get to the "prize" inside.

But life is not the prize inside the wrapper. **Life is the tearing.** When you spend Seven years tearing away the moments to get to the trophies, you wake up to find you have a shelf full of gold and a trash can full of lived experiences. You have become a billionaire of "Possibility" and a beggar of "Presence." I was "Winning," but I was not **Living.**

Imagine the Roman general returning from a campaign. He has the gold. He has the slaves. He has the laurel wreath pressed against his brow. But when he returns to his villa, the rooms are silent. The people he conquered for are gone.

This is where the philosophy stops being a lecture and starts being a wound.

Standing in my room after the deaths of my maternal uncle, my father, and finally, my mother—the three pillars of my reality—I felt the weight of that Roman silence. I had the "Conquests"—those twenty-three awards. I had the "Rank"—the Grammy voting membership. But the room where my mother used to clap was hollow. The phone that used to ring with my uncle's emotional voice, vibrating with the raw connection of a new song, was still.

The tragic irony of my greed was this: I was writing songs to find love, but the process of chasing the success of those songs made me a ghost to the people who already loved me perfectly. I was so busy writing about the "Muse" that I forgot to be the "Son." I was so busy aiming for the "Future" that I missed the "Now" that was sitting in the kitchen, waiting for me to just sit down and have tea. It's not that I didn't spend time with them or that I didn't love them. But when I look back now, I can't help feeling that I could have done more... that I could have been better.

I had been so lost in reaching for more heights that I forgot to inhabit the base of the mountain. I was chasing a future I never caught, and in the process, I failed to stay in the present that was already mine.

There is a subtle violence in constant ambition. It is a violence against the self. To be perpetually "leaning forward" is to tell your current self that you are not enough. It is a quiet, persistent rejection of the man sitting in the chair right now.

Seneca argued that "the greatest obstacle to living is expectancy, which hangs upon tomorrow and loses today." Every time I sat in my studio, obsessing over a lyric—not for the pure joy of the vibration, but for the validation it might bring—I was committing a micro-aggression against my own peace. I was telling my mother's applause, "Your love is beautiful, but I need the world's love to feel real." I was labeling the "Present" as **Insufficient** and the "Future" as **Salvation**.

Greed is the belief that external accumulation can fill an internal void. But the void isn't a hole that needs filling; it's a room that needs **inhabiting.** We keep throwing awards and accolades into the room, hoping the space will disappear. But the space remains, and now it's just crowded with clutter we don't have the time to dust.

Let us look at this without "good" or "bad" labels. **Greed is an engine.** In Seneca's era, it was the hunger for expansion that built the aqueducts that still stand today. In our world, it is the spark that turns a dream into forty songs. It is the fuel of ambition. It is absolutely needed to motivate us; it is the fire that pushes us to see what we are capable of. Without that "leaning forward," the human story would be a stagnant pond.

The "Bad" label we give greed is usually just our fear of the fire. But the "Good" label we give ambition is often just our denial of the smoke.

The truth is neutral: Greed is a biological and psychological propellant. It is the part of you that refuses to settle. The issue isn't the hunger; it's the **identification** with the hunger. When you are the hunger, you are a slave. When you observe the hunger, you are an artist.

Staying grounded while the fire of ambition burns—this is the true mastery. It is what the Stoics called Ataraxia—a state of serene calmness even in the midst of the storm.

It is the ability to work for the achievement while knowing that the achievement will never "complete" you. It is knowing that the 24th award will feel exactly like the 1st—a momentary spike followed by a return to the same self you've been avoiding.

Nothing is enough... not because nothing is substantial... but because nothing is inhabited. Satisfaction becomes a ghost; it dissolves the second you touch it because your mind has already moved the goalposts another mile down the track.

Today, the "pulse" of greed still hums in my chest. It hasn't gone away, and I no longer wish for it to. It is the energy I use to create. But I have changed my relationship to it.

When I feel that pressure behind my eyes—the "leaning forward" that wants to skip over the current song to see how it will be received—I stop. I look at the walls of my studio. I remember the clap that is no longer there. I remember the phone call that will never come again.

I realize that the future I was chasing is a ghost, and the only thing that has any flavor at all is the note I am playing right now.

Greed is the fuel, but Presence is the destination. If you don't arrive today, you will never arrive. You can have twenty-three awards on the shelf, but if you aren't there to feel the wood of the shelf beneath your fingers, you are still a beggar.

The only real wealth is the ability to stand in the wreckage of your own life, amidst the silence and the trophies, and say: "I am here. And for right now, this is enough." We suffer maximum in our imagination because greed tells us we are "missing out." But in reality, the only thing we ever miss out on is the moment we refuse to inhabit. Break the label of "Success," and you find the truth of **Being.**

"Greed is the arithmetic of a ghost; it tries to fill a hole in the 'Being' with the weight of the 'Having.' You are chasing a horizon that moves only because you do, forgetting that you are already standing on the earth you seek."

Chapter 5:
The God-Bias

There are moments in a human life where nothing external is broken, and yet, something inside simply stops working. It isn't a violent crash; it's a quiet, irreversible shift—like a complex machine that begins to fail while its gears are still polished and spinning.

Before the first doctrine is whispered into your ear, before the word "Sin" even exists in your vocabulary, your body moves with a terrifying, beautiful directness. A rhythm appears, and your feet follow. A sound emerges, and your voice responds without checking a map. You reach for the world because the world is there to be touched.

In this state, there is no division. There is no "Observer" standing over the experience with a stopwatch and a gavel. There is only the movement. Only the response.

And then, the layer is added.

This new layer doesn't originate from your nerves or your gut. It sits over the body. It is a voice that carries authority not because it is felt, but because it is believed. It is the **God-Bias**. It is the internal judge that walks into the room of your soul and begins slapping labels on everything that moves: This is pure. That is wrong. This is allowed. That is forbidden.

I saw this mechanical failure most clearly during a journey through the Middle East. I met a woman who was, by every natural metric, a masterpiece of elegance and grace. Her walk, her talk—everything about her moved with a rhythm that felt ancient and honest. We began to lean into each other. It wasn't a calculation; it was a response.

But she lived in a world where the internal compass had been replaced by a map drawn by others. She was a daughter of a rigid doctrine, and I was a son of the wind. As our liking deepened into something more profound, the God-Bias began its silent, steady work. Her heart was calling for me, but her ears were ringing with the sound of "Forbidden."

For ten months, I tried to show her the world outside of her "don'ts." I watched her slowly begin to trust her own will. She tried things she had been told were "Sinful"—small joys, simple freedoms—and her body responded with delight. In those moments, the system aligned. The breath deepened. The chest opened. She was, for a fraction of time, **un-divided.**

But the God-Bias does not leave its subjects easily. It waits for the moment of truth to reassert its grip.

When the time came to bring our reality into the light—to tell her family—the interruption arrived. Her sister didn't ask what I did for a living or how I treated people. She asked the only question the script allowed:

"Do you think our father will accept this? It is not according to the scriptures."

In that single sentence, ten months of shared breath, shared laughter, and shared truth were tossed into the dustbin. It didn't take a year of contemplation. It took a single minute of fear.

She repented instantly—not because she had done something wrong, but because she was terrified. The label of "Sin" carried more weight than the reality of "Love." I sat there and watched a "handicapped" person. Her heart was crying out for me, reaching through her eyes, but her hands were tied by invisible threads of doctrine.

This is the heartbreak of the God-Bias. It is not an emotion; it is a **mechanical failure.** The system that was built for connection was overridden by a system built for obedience. She sacrificed the living man for the dead ink.

Why does the heart surrender so quickly? We like to think of "God" as a distant, cosmic entity, but the God-Bias is far more local. It is the **Ghost-Army of the Tribe.**

When she looked at the possibility of a life with me, she wasn't just looking at a man; she was looking at the threat of **Exile**. For a human being, exile is a form of death. For thousands of years, to be cast out of the tribe meant you would perish in the wilderness. We have evolved to fear the disapproval of the "Father" or the "Priest" more than we value the satisfaction of our own souls.

Behind her sister's question stood a thousand years of ancestors, all nodding in unison, all pointing their fingers at the "Different." The Scripture is the heavy, leather-bound contract that keeps the tribe together. If she broke the contract for me, she would lose her history, her safety, and her name.

The "God-Bias" isn't about morality; it's about **Belonging.** We are so greedy for the "Security" of the group that we are willing to murder our own authenticity to keep our seat at the table. She didn't choose God; she chose the **Gaze of the Group.** She preferred the "Cage of the Known" over the "Freedom of the Individual," because freedom feels too much like being alone in the dark.

We have been taught that anything that changes is unreliable. Our feelings are labeled as "fickle," our desires as "temporary." To combat this uncertainty, we are told to anchor ourselves to the Scripture. We label the "Written" as **Eternal** and the "Felt" as **Dangerous.**

Scripture is the ultimate anchor. It is designed to keep the world static. It is a war against Change. And because Love is the ultimate catalyst for change, the Scripture must always seek to contain it, to border it, and—if it cannot control it—to kill it.

We have been conditioned to believe that if a truth is written in a book, it is a "Law," but if a truth is written in our own heartbeat, it is a "Temptation." This creates a hierarchy where a dead letter from the past is given more authority than a living pulse in the present. **We worship the menu instead of eating the meal.**

What is the legacy of such a choice?

When a woman stops loving because she is afraid of a book, she is not moving closer to God; she is suffering a breakdown of her natural systems. She has allowed a "Foreign Script" to overwrite her "Original Code."

I saw her posture change in that final moment. The elegance and grace didn't leave her, but they stiffened. She became a statue of her own belief system. When she looked at me that last time, she wasn't looking at a man she loved; she was looking at a "Deviation." I wasn't fighting a man; I was fighting a **Wall of Words.**

The legacy of the "God-Bias" is a life lived in **Muffled Tones.** It is the sound of a song played through a thick velvet curtain. You can hear the melody, but you can never feel the vibration.

After she left, I felt the residue of that choice in my own music. I began to ask myself: Am I writing this song to be "Good" (the label), or am I writing it to be "True" (the reality)? I realized that we all carry a "Handicapped" version of ourselves—a version that has been told that its natural signals are "Bad." We spend our lives "Correcting" our beauty until it is unrecognizable.

In the "No-Label" world, there is no "different religion." There is only the frequency of one human being meeting another. She wasn't choosing "God" over me. She was choosing a **label of God** over the experience of God. If the Divine is anything, it is the flow of life, the unconflicted rhythm of the heart, the grace of an elegant walk. By choosing the script, she didn't move closer to the sacred—she moved away from the only sacred thing we actually have: **The truth of the present moment.**

When you lose trust in your own sensation, you don't just lose your partner. You lose the connection to the self that was never divided to begin with. You become a ghost haunting your own ribcage, waiting for a permission that will never come from a voice that was never yours to begin with.

We suffer maximum in our imagination because we imagine that God is a bookkeeper, tallying up our deviations from the script. We label our natural desires as "Bad" and our artificial constraints as "Good." We create a world where a woman will starve her own soul to satisfy a definition of "Purity" that has no heartbeat.

The abyss she feared wasn't the "Outside"—the abyss was the hollow silence of a life lived by someone else's rules. The only sin is the one we commit against our own "Original Code." Break the label, and you find that the "God" you were so afraid of was actually the one calling you to love in the first place.

"We have built a God in the image of our own tremors and called it 'Faith.' But a Creator who weaves the galaxies does not require your fear; he requires your presence. Stop reading the menu and start eating the feast."

Part III
The Neutral Practice

Chapter 6:
The Clinical Eye

Before the heart can be healed, the eyes must be retrained. We have spent our lives looking through a stained-glass window of "Good," "Bad," "Holy," and "Sinful." We don't see the world; we see our opinions of it. We don't experience a person; we experience our expectations of them. To break the cage, we must learn the art of the **Clinical Eye.** We must learn to see the thing itself, stripped of the story we've been told to tell about it.

Sit with an object. Do not name it. The moment the word "Stone" or "Watch" enters your mind, you have stopped seeing. You have filed it away in a drawer of "Things I already know." Do not identify it. Let the first impulse to recognize it pass without following it.

Now, begin.

A form is positioned on a horizontal surface. Estimate its length. Measure it visually, using your hand or a nearby reference. Observe the width at its widest point. Stay with what can be seen. Notice the surface. There are layers. Thin structures extend outward from a central mass. Observe their direction. Their density.

Do not say what they are. Move your attention to color. Not what the color represents—not the "Red" of anger or the "White" of purity. Only what is present. Segments of dark tone. Areas of lighter distribution. Irregular patterns where one tone transitions into another. Do not call it beautiful. Do not call it damaged. Let color exist without a conclusion.

Observe the structure. There is a central axis. From it, extensions project outward. Measure them with your eyes. Compare one side to the other. Is there asymmetry? Stay with observation. Look at the edges. Some lines are continuous. Others break. Notice where continuity stops.

Bring your attention to the surface beneath. There is contact. Points of pressure. Slight displacement of particles. Indentation where mass meets ground. Observe how the form interacts with what supports it.

Now, pause. Notice what the mind is trying to do. It is panicking. It is desperate to name. It wants to conclude. It wants to tell you what this is so it can stop looking at it. It wants to wrap the object in a label: “This is a dead bird,” or “This is a broken toy.”

Do not follow that movement.

Return to what is visible. Observe stillness. There is no motion. No expansion. No contraction. Only position. Remain here for a few moments longer. Without labeling. Without meaning. Only color. Only texture. Only measurement. This is the beginning of seeing without the inherited lens. Not what the object is... but what is actually there.

Society is a collection of scripts. We have a script for birth, a script for success, and a very rigid, black-ink script for death. We are told that when a pillar of our life collapses, the "Correct" response is a total systemic failure. We label the tears as **Respect** and the silence as **Coldness.**

But let us apply the Clinical Eye to the day my world became quiet.

I was in the kitchen when the news of my maternal uncle’s death arrived.

I was standing near a heat source. I was consuming the flesh of a fish. My jaw was moving in a rhythmic, mechanical motion. The flavor was salt and oil.

A phone call arrived. A series of sound waves carrying information: The heart has stopped. The breath has ceased. Mass has become still. For the world, the label would be: "He was eating fish while his uncle died. How heartless." But through the Clinical Eye, there is no "Heartlessness." There is only a biological body requiring fuel, and another biological body reaching the end of its duration. The fish was still a fish. The hunger was still a hunger. The death was a fact, not a disruption of the laws of physics.

When my mother died—the woman whose applause once defined my world—I performed the last rites. I moved my limbs, I spoke the words, I handled the remains. I did not hide from the reality of the dust.

And then, I went home. I ate biryani. I lay down on a horizontal surface, and I slept.

To the "God-Bias" of society (Chapter 5), this is a sin. I saw the narrowed eyes of the mourners. I heard the hushed whispers of people who had spent months ignoring her while she was alive, but who were now performing a symphony of grief. They looked at my "Normal" behavior and projected their own fear onto me. They needed me to be "Broken" so they could feel "Good."

Foreheads wrinkled. Eyes damp. Mouths turned downward in a scripted arc. Their grief was a performance for an invisible audience. My lack of tears was a mechanical reality.

The body does not read the "Grief Script." The body only knows that it has been through a massive expenditure of energy and it requires restoration. Eating is not "Dishonor"; it is a biological necessity. Sleeping is not "Apathy"; it is the nervous system resetting after a peak event.

Why do people cry so loudly at funerals? Often, it is not for the dead. The dead have no more "Pulse of Fear." They have no "Hunger of Greed." They have arrived at the ultimate neutrality.

The tears are often for the **Unfinished Business.** They are the result of a life lived through the "Temporal Stutter" of Chapter 4—always leaning into the future, always ignoring the person sitting at the table, until that person is gone. The loud mourning is the sound of **Regret.** It is the "Imaginary Suffering" of realizing you traded the Real (the presence) for the Label (the distraction).

I didn't cry because I didn't have to.

For years, while they were breathing, I was present. We occupied the same space. We exchanged sound waves. We shared nutrients. We celebrated the "Now." Because I had already "Eaten the Meal" while it was hot, I didn't need to cry over the empty plate.

If you can look at your own pain with a Clinical Eye, it loses its ability to crush you.

Instead of *"I am a failure,"* you see: A heavy sensation in the chest. A downward curve of the mouth. A slowing of the heart rate.

Instead of *"I am heartbroken,"* you see: A rhythmic tightening in the throat. A displacement of tears. A memory-loop playing in the frontal lobe.

When I looked at my 23 awards with a Clinical Eye, I didn't see "Success." I saw gold-plated mass. I saw light reflecting off a curved surface. When the labels fell away, the "Greed" lost its power.

When I looked at death with a Clinical Eye, I saw that it is simply the cessation of a rhythm. It is not "Bad." It is an inevitable segment of a continuous line. I allowed my parents to leave peacefully. I didn't tether them to the earth with the "Greed" of my own mourning. I let the form become still, and I let my own form continue its movement.

Not what the object means... but what is actually there.

This is the only way out of the cage. To see the bars not as "Evil," but as "Vertical lines of iron." Once they are just lines, you can begin to find the space between them.

To eat your biryani and sleep when the world tells you to starve and weep is not an act of cruelty. It is an act of **Sovereignty.** It is the moment you realize the "Cage" was only made of other people's labels. You are finally seeing with your own eyes. You are finally un-muffled.

"The truth does not require your emotional consent to exist. To possess the Clinical Eye is to stop asking why the storm is happening and to start measuring the wind. Reality is only 'Cruel' to those who are still clutching a lie."

Chapter 7: Love as an Unblinking Mirror

They sit across from each other. No words pass between them. The space is not empty—it is a live wire of observation—but it is undisturbed. One body carries visible strain. The shoulders are collapsed inward, a physical closing of the gates. The breath is a mechanical struggle—shallow, then abruptly deep, then restrained. The **God-Bias** from Chapter 5 is standing over the lungs with a stopwatch, timing every expansion to ensure it stays within the "Allowed" limits.

Across from this, another body remains. Spine upright, but not rigid. Breath consistent, unforced. The eyes are open—not searching for a "Good" side, not analyzing a "Bad' side, and crucially, not avoiding the "Ugly" side.

This is the **Unblinking Mirror.**

When I first met her in the Middle East, my **Clinical Eye** (Chapter 6) saw the data immediately. I saw a woman with a potential so exceptional it felt like a frequen cy from another world. Her grace wasn't just aesthetic; it was a rhythmic intelligence. But I also saw the chains. I saw twenty-eight years of "Don'ts." I saw a human being whose every natural impulse was being strangled by the ink of ancient scriptures.

My first reaction was the typical one. it was the **Greed to Fix.** I tried to go down the path of logic. I tried to tell her, "What you are doing is not good for you. This doctrine is a cage. You are wasting your light."

But look at the mechanics of that interaction: By telling her she was "Wrong," I was just becoming another version of her Father. I was another man with a "Script" telling her how to exist. My values were "Better" in my eyes, but to her soul, I was just another source of pressure. I was leaning forward, trying to reshape her, and in response, she did what every caged thing does: **She stiffened.** I was trying to "Enlighten" her, but I was actually just competing for the position of her Jailer.

True enlightenment is not the addition of new information; it is the subtraction of interference.

As **Kahlil Gibran** suggests, the soul does not walk upon a line, neither does it grow like a reed. The soul unfolds itself, like a lotus of countless petals. When we try to "Save" someone by imposing our own ideology, we are essentially trying to pull the petals open with our fingers. We destroy the bloom in our haste to see the flower.

I realized then that twenty-eight years of reinforcement cannot be undone by an argument. You cannot talk a person out of a prison they believe is a sanctuary. The only way to dissolve a label is to provide a **Reality** that contradicts it. I had to stop being a "Teacher" and start being a "Space."

I stopped the "Corrective" talk. I stopped the ideology. Instead, I became the Mirror.

I invited her to experience the "Forbidden." I didn't tell her it was "Good"; I simply allowed it to be **Present.** At first, the resistance was massive. The God-Bias screamed in her ears. She refused. She recoiled. She looked at the "Don'ts" as if they were pits of fire. But because I didn't withdraw—because I remained like the mountain, unblinking and non-judgmental—she eventually found the curiosity to step across the line.

She began to experience the things her book called "Sin." She tasted the freedoms she had been taught were "Dark."

And then, the internal revolution occurred. **The body recognized the truth.**

The moment she felt the joy of a "Forbidden" experience, the label "Sin" lost its mass. It became a hollow word. Her perspective didn't broaden because I gave her a lecture; it broadened because her own sensory reality overrode her inherited script. The **Original Code** (Chapter 5) recognized the light.

To love a person is to help them find the "Unblinking Mirror" within themselves. Every soul is born with a **Natural Calling**—a unique gift, a specific "Sound" that it is meant to contribute to the symphony of existence. But we spend our lives muffling that sound to fit the "Script."

When you love someone, you act as a buffer against that suppression. You create a "Laboratory of the Unallowed" where they can test their wings without fear of being shot down. You aren't "Fixing" them; you are simply removing the weights from their ankles.

In that room of stillness, when I sat with her, I wasn't looking at her "Flaws." I was looking at her **Potential**. I was seeing the "Asymmetry" of her life and refusing to call it a "Problem." I was providing the silence necessary for her suppressed gifts to stir.

Nothing was solved by my words. But everything was allowed by my presence.

This is the ultimate form of Love. It is a presence that does not blink, even when what it sees has been called "Broken" by the rest of the world.

Society tells us to avoid the "Broken," or to pity them, or to fix them. But the "No-Label" partner knows that "Brokenness" is just a label for **Transformation.** When you stop labeling your partner, your child, or your friend as "Someone who needs to be saved," you finally give them the space to **Save Themselves.**

In the "No-Label" world, Love is not a transaction. It is not an emotion that seeks a response. It is a state of **Sovereignty.** It is the ability to say:

"I see your chains. I see your twenty-eight years of 'No.' I am not going to fight your chains. I am just going to stand here and love the woman underneath them until she realizes they were never locked."

Nothing has been said. Nothing has been forced. And yet, the world has become larger. The "Natural Calling" has been heard. The "Handicapped" soul is learning to walk, not because someone gave it a crutch, but because it realized it was never actually broken—it was only **Belabeled.**

This is the ending of the war. You stop being the jailer, and you stop being the liberator. You simply become the Mirror. And in that reflection, the other person finally sees what you've seen all along: That they are, and have always been, enough. The "God-Bias" falls away, leaving only the "Natural Calling"—the sound of a soul finally permitted to be itself.

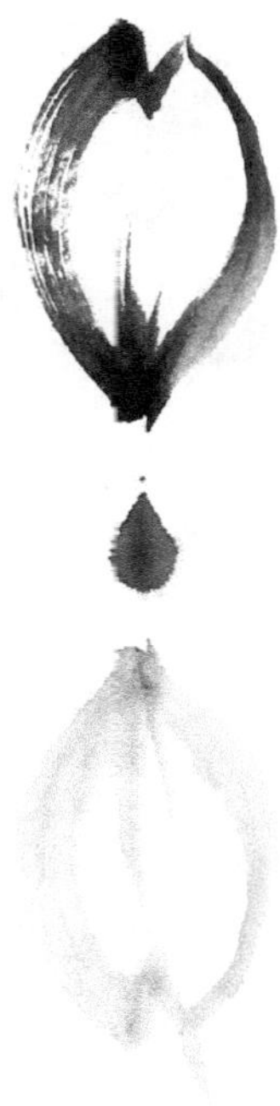

"To love is not to 'fix' the other; it is to hold a mirror so still and so Neutral that they finally see the 'Original Code' they have spent a lifetime hiding. You do not change them; you simply refuse to believe in their cage."

Part IV
The Functioning Will

Chapter 8: The Residue (What Remains)

When the labels fall away, they do not announce their departure with a fanfare or a grand declaration of independence. There is no cinematic moment where the mind suddenly shouts, "I am free!" Conditioning is not a wall that you knock down; it is a fog that thins so gradually you don't realize it's gone until you notice you can see the horizon.

There is only a quiet absence. A space where something that was always speaking is finally no longer being interrupted.

At first, this silence feels unfamiliar, even threatening. Not because it is new, but because it has never been allowed to stand on its own without the **God-Bias** (Chapter 5) or the **Clinical Eye** (Chapter 6) hovering over it. There is no instruction attached to this silence. No approval waiting at the end. No consequence shaping its direction.

There is only a movement.

It begins in the body. Not as a thought, not as a decision, but as a subtle, magnetic pull. If your attention is still searching for "Meaning" or "Purpose," you will miss it. This movement does not explain itself. It does not justify its existence to your intellect. It simply leans in a direction.

The body responds before the mind can organize a defense. The breath changes—not because you are practicing a "Technique," but because the lungs have finally been given the space they didn't know they needed.

Observe the shift in posture. It isn't "Corrected" by a therapist or a coach; it is **Aligned** by nature.

- The spine lengthens without effort.
- The shoulders drop without a mental instruction to "relax."
- The muscles engage not from tension, but from **Participation.**

This is the first sign of the Residue: **The absence of friction.** In your 23-award climb (Chapter 4), every movement was friction. You were pushing against the world, pushing against your own fatigue, pushing for the next height. But in the Residue, the movement follows a path of zero resistance.

The hands begin to do something—perhaps they reach for the keys of the piano, or they begin to cook a meal, or they simply rest—not because they should, but because they are already moving.

For years, my brain functioned like a high-speed processor programmed for one task: **Optimization.** Whenever someone I loved shared something with me—a fear, a dream, a simple observation—my mind would immediately switch into "Mode." Before they could even finish their sentence, I was already three steps ahead, calculating: What is wrong here? What is the solution? How can I repair this? I labeled their words as "Problems" and my intervention as "Love." But in reality, I wasn't listening. I was **Greedily** reaching for a conclusion. I was a "Fixer" who was too busy building a bridge to realize that the person just wanted to stand in the river with me.

The Residue is what remains when that "Fixer" finally dies. Now, when I sit with a loved one, I don't hunt for answers. I don't try to find the "Correct" response. I just listen. I absorb. I learn. I have stopped treating human connection like a technical glitch that needs a patch. I treat it like a frequency to be tuned into.

Most of our life's greatest work does not come from "Grinding" or "Hustling." It comes when you learn to stay calm, silent, and idle.

Society labels "Doing Nothing" as **Laziness.** It labels "Silence" as **Awkwardness.** But through the Clinical Eye, we see that "Doing Nothing" is the most active state of the brain. When you stop judging, stop fixing, and stop labeling, your brain opens in a thousand different directions at once.

A simple talk with a loved one, met with an empty mind, can become a doorway to a new universe of thought. But for that to happen, you must learn to think nothing. You must become the **Unblinking Mirror** (Chapter 7) for yourself.

In my studio now, the air feels different. The ghosts of "Success" and "Validation" have been evicted.

I sit at the keys, and the "Click" happens almost immediately. Why? Because I am no longer reaching for a "Recognition" or "Awards." I am not performing for my mother's applause or my uncle's pride. Those voices were beautiful, but they were **Interference.** When I play now, I am simply following the pattern that was always there. The Residue is a creative state where the sound doesn't come from me; it happens through me. There is no awareness of progress. No checking if the melody is "Right" or "Wrong." There is only the vibration of air and the movement of fingers.

When you first strip away the labels of "Successful Musician" or "Grateful Son," there is a moment of sheer vertigo. The mind panics. It feels like falling into a void. We have been so conditioned to define ourselves by our **attachments** (Chapter 4) and our **doctrines** (Chapter 5) that when they vanish, we feel like we are disappearing.

But this vertigo is the birth of **Sovereignty.**

In the Residue, you realize that you do not need a name to exist. You do not need a "Story" to be valid. The "God-Bias" told you that you were a "Sinner" or a "Saint." The "Greed" told you that you were a "Winner" or a "Loser." The **Clinical Eye** (Chapter 6) shows you the truth: You are a **Biological Event.** You are a localized frequency of life.

Most people spend their lives trying to be "High"—vibrating at the frequency of excitement, praise, or peak performance. But the Residue is the **Frequency of the Neutral.**

Neutrality is not "Boredom." Neutrality is **Infinite Potential.** When you are neutral, you are like a blank canvas that doesn't care what color is splashed upon it. You can experience the death of a loved one without the "Grief Script" (Chapter 6) because you aren't trying to maintain a "Label" of being a good person. You can experience a massive success without the "Greed for More" because you aren't trying to maintain a "Label" of being a winner.

The Residue is the ability to walk through the world and let things **Pass Through You.** * **Praise** arrives; it passes through.

- Insult arrives; it passes through.
- Loss arrives; it passes through.

Nothing sticks because there are no "Label-Hooks" left for the world to grab onto. You have become "Slippery" to the cage.

This is what remains when the labels dissolve: **The absence of contradiction.** Nothing inside is pulling in the opposite direction. Nothing is asking for this moment to be something else. There is no voice interrupting the act with correction, evaluation, or the "Greed for More" (Chapter 4).

If you are eating biryani after a death, eat. If you are sitting in silence with a partner, listen. If you are writing a song that will never be heard, play.

To live in the Residue is to finally inhabit your own life. You realize that the "Cage" was never made of iron bars; it was made of the **Descriptions** of the bars.

- **Fear** was just a name for a biological tightening.
- **Greed** was just a name for a temporal displacement.
- **Sin** was just a name for an ancestral rule.

Once you stop describing them, you find that there is nothing to solve. There is only the "Original Code"—a system that is already perfect in its neutrality. You don't need to be "Good." You don't need to be "Successful." You don't even need to be "Happy."

You only need to be **Present.**

The journey of "No Labels" is not a journey toward a destination. It is a journey of **Arrival in the Now.**

It is the realization that the "Cage" was a ghost. The "Fear" was a phantom. The "Greed" was a shadow. And the "Labels" were just ink on a map that had nothing to do with the actual land.

Now, I sit in my studio. The air is still. The keyboard is under my fingers. A loved one is speaking in the next room. I am not a "Fixer." I am not a "Winner." I am not a "Sinner."

I am just the **Doing.**

I am just the **Listening.**

I am just the **Being.**

Nothing has been added.

Nothing has been removed.

The interference has stopped.

And for the first time in my life, I am not reaching for the "Next."

I am finally, undeniably, **Here.**

"When the labels are burned away and the 'God-Bias' is silenced, you do not become nothing. You become the Source.
The Residue is the only part of you that was never a script; it is the silent apex that remains when the noise of the world finally breaks."

Chapter 9:
The Daily Debridement

The room is already divided before a single word is spoken. It isn't the furniture or the walls; it's the undercurrents. Opinions move through the air like invisible silk threads, pulling people into alignment without a single announcement. We are tribal animals. Our ancient **Pulse of Fear** (Chapter 3) tells us that to be alone is to be prey, so we instinctively sniff out the "Side" that will keep us safe.

You enter. No one asks you to choose a side immediately, but the expectation is a physical weight. It lives in the way a conversation pauses just a fraction of a second when you arrive. It's in the way eyes measure your posture before you've opened your mouth. They aren't looking for you; they are looking for your **Label.**

I see this every day. I see people fighting for labels—political parties, religious superiority, geopolitical stances—yet 99% of them cannot tell you why they are fighting. They aren't driven by data; they are driven by the **Herd Mentality.**

I once watched a video of a protest regarding a tense geopolitical situation between Iran and the USA. The protestor was vocal, passionate, and certain. She was opposing the USA's actions and supporting the leadership in Iran. But when the interviewer asked a simple, Clinical question—*"What specifically is the USA doing wrong according to you?"*—the system failed.

There were no details. No facts. Only surface-level echoes: "They've been doing wrong for so many years... this and that." When pressed for a single concrete detail, she had no answer. She wasn't protesting a policy; she was wearing a **Label** as an armor. She didn't have a "Calling"; she had a "Category."

The same phenomenon appeared in India when a leader in Iran passed away. Suddenly, the local community "awakened." I saw it through a close friend's phone—her entire WhatsApp list was flooded with status updates supporting a leader many had likely never heard of the day before. In one night, a stranger became a saint.

Why? Because the **Tribe** (Chapter 3) demanded a signal. To post the status was to say, "I am one of you." To stay silent was to risk being "Outside." This is the **God-Bias** (Chapter 5) in its social form: we don't look at the human being; we look at the banner they are standing under.

We suffer from the "Greed for a Hero." We want to believe that because a Prime Minister, a President, or a Religious Leader did one "Good" thing, every action they take must be perfect. We label them as **Saints** or **Saviors**, and in doing so, we blind ourselves to the other side of the coin.

Through the **Clinical Eye**, we see the truth: Everyone—whether it's you, me, or the leader of a nation—is a biological system capable of both "Good" and "Bad" actions. That is the fundamental nature of being human. No one knows what will happen tomorrow. No one has a monopoly on the "Right Way."

To have **Blind Faith** in a leader is to commit a mechanical error. It is to stop observing and start obeying. The "No-Label" partner says: *"He did something good, I see that. Now, let me see the other side of the coin. Let me look at the data before I reach a conclusion."*

You stand in a room full of these "Awakened" certainties. Someone turns to you. They offer a question that is actually a doorway. *"You've seen this, right? You agree?"*

In that moment, your body prepares for battle. Your chest tightens. Your mind starts scanning its "Scripture" or its "Greed for Approval" to find the "Correct" response. The social pressure acts like a gravitational pull, urging you to settle the tension by picking a side.

But you do nothing.

You let the breath finish. You look at the person—not as a representative of a "Side," but as a biological form. You see the forward lean of their body. You see the impatience in their eyes. You recognize that their "Certainty" is just a mask for their Fear.

"I hear what you're saying."

The sentence lands, but it does not attach. It returns the words without absorbing their heat. You have refused the label. You have stayed in the **Residue** (Chapter 8).

In medicine, debridement is the removal of dead tissue so that the healthy part can heal. **The Daily Debridement** is the psychological equivalent. Every day, the world tries to graft its labels onto you. If you don't clear them away, they become your skin.

The practice is a deliberate return to the **Immediate:**

- Observe the hand moving as someone speaks.
- Hear the tremor in a voice that carries its "Certainty" too tightly.
- See the "God-Bias" acting as a filter between two people.

Nothing is reduced. Nothing is fixed. And slowly, the pressure to take a side loses its hold. Not because the sides have disappeared, but because they are no longer required for your survival. You have realized that you don't need to be "Right" to be "Real."

Time passes. The room remains divided. But inside you, there is no accumulation. No weight of opposition. No identity formed through alignment.

You move through the world like a "Slippery" object. The hooks of the Herd find nothing to grab onto. You remain among the same voices, but you are **untouched** by the need to become one of them. You are finally a **Sovereign System.**

The Daily Debridement is the realization that peace is not the absence of conflict in the world; it is the absence of conflict **with the world.** When you stop labeling people as "Opponents" or "Allies," you finally see them as they are: human beings caught in a "Temporal Stutter," reaching for a safety that doesn't exist.

You become the **Unblinking Mirror** (Chapter 7) even in a room full of shouting. Every label that tries to settle is seen, acknowledged, and allowed to pass. What remains is only the **Residue**: the quiet, undeniable alignment of a soul that has finally stopped fighting for a side and started living for the **Now.**

"Debridement is not a one-time event;
it is the daily hygiene of the Sovereign. You must be
willing to cut away the 'Labels' as fast as the world tries
to stick them to your skin. If it does not belong to the
'Original Code,' it has no business in the body."

Chapter 10:
The World Restored

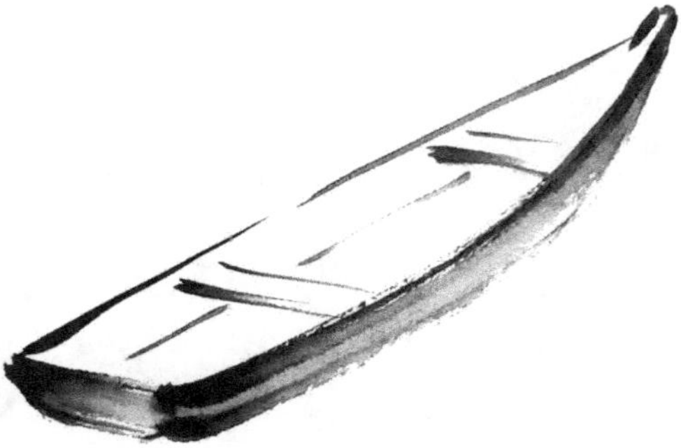

There is a way of seeing that returns—not as a new skill you have labored to build, but as a landscape uncovered after a long storm. It does not arrive with effort. It does not require construction. It is simply what remains when you stop trying to hold the world in place with your own hands.

Step back.

Do not move your feet; move your perception. Let the frame widen beyond your name, beyond your 23 awards, beyond your grief, and beyond the "God-Bias" that has policed your every breath. Let the frame widen until the personal becomes the universal.

Before you were a "Son," a "Musician," or a "Sinner," you were an event in the dark.

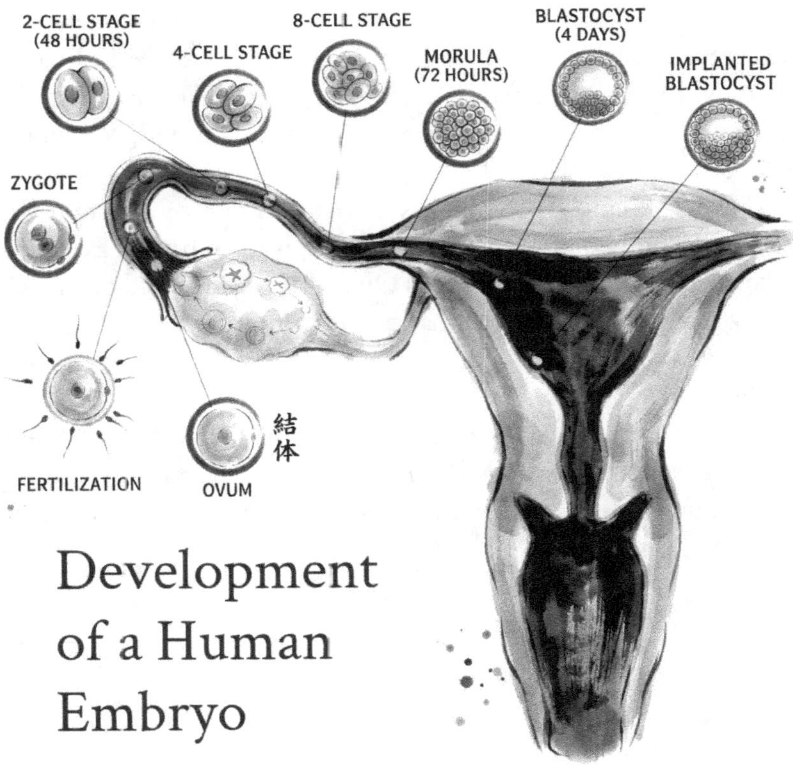

Development of a Human Embryo

Inside the womb, cells divided in absolute silence. Structures assembled themselves without a single instruction from a textbook or a scripture. Your heart began to move—a rhythmic thump established without your permission and without your help. This was the "Original Code" (Chapter 5) in its purest state. Breath entered your lungs not as a "Decision," but as a biological event.

Growth did not announce itself. It accumulated. Your bones lengthened, your skin stretched, and your neural pathways strengthened through the simple repetition of being alive. Sensation eventually became interpretation, and interpretation became the "Identity" that you spent the next few decades trying to protect. You attached a name to this biological miracle and began to treat the miracle like a business that needed to be "Successful.

Alongside this formation, the "Breakdown" was already present. This is the truth the "Pulse of Fear" (Chapter 3) tries to hide: Decay is not an ending that happens later; it is a process that is happening now. Cells replace themselves. Structures weaken and rebuild. Nothing holds its shape permanently.

What we label as "Stable" is actually a state of constant, frantic change. When you look at your life through the **Clinical Eye** (Chapter 6), you see that you aren't a "Fixed Object" trying to avoid death; you are a **Flow** that is death and birth happening simultaneously.

Step back further.

Observe the movement of bodies across the surface of the earth. Some move fast, driven by the "Hunger of Greed" (Chapter 4). Some move slow, weighted down by "Grief" (Chapter 6). Some are rising; some are falling.

Carbon Cycle

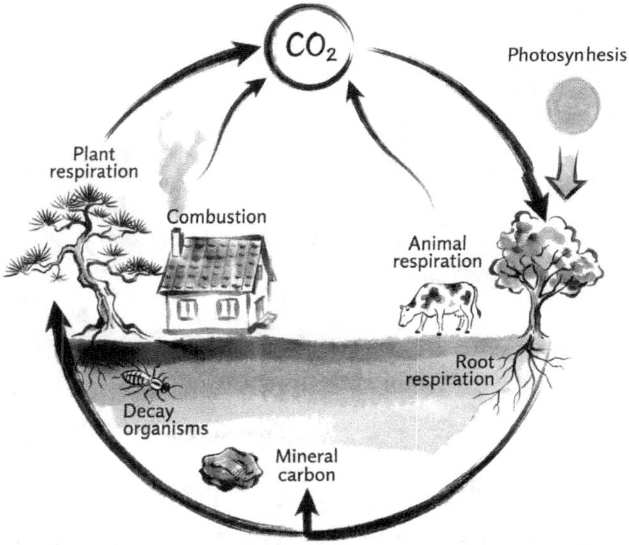

But from this height, no single movement exists in isolation. Each is part of a larger pattern that does not center around you. A leaf unfolds, holds its shape briefly, and then returns to the ground. A building is constructed, used, abandoned, and reclaimed by the elements. A sound—perhaps one of your forty songs—is made, heard, and eventually forgotten.

Nothing in nature resists its own transition. The leaf does not scream when it turns brown. The stars do not panic when they collapse. Only the human mind, armed with its labels of "Good" and "Bad," resists the flow of the universe.

Step further still.

The very ground beneath you, which you labeled as "Solid," is rearranging itself over eons. Layers move beneath layers. The stars above hold their positions relative to each other, then drift. Patterns emerge, dissolve, and re-emerge in different arrangements. Cycles repeat, not exactly, but continuously.

The motion of the universe does not pause for your approval. It does not ask to be understood. It does not require "Meaning" (Chapter 8). Within all of this, there is **Awareness**. Not as something separate from what is seen—not as a "Soul" that is trapped in a "Body"—but as the very condition that allows anything to be seen at all.

- Birth occurs.
- Decay occurs.
- Movement continues.

Nothing is outside of this. There is no "God-Bias" standing apart to control it. The need to define begins to loosen here, not because definitions are "Wrong," but because they are **Unnecessary.** What is does not require your agreement.

When you reach this perspective, there is no position left to defend. There is no identity to stabilize. There is no belief that must be protected from contradiction because you have realized that you are the contradiction.

You are a body breathing. Not as "My" breath, but as **Breath occurring.** You are a vibration of air. Not as "My" music, but as **Sound passing through space.** You are a thought appearing, holding briefly, and dissolving.

Everything is happening without needing to be held. And in that realization, something settles. It isn't the "Excitement" of Chapter 4 or the "Repentance" of Chapter 5. It is the **Absence of Tension.** Because nothing is being resisted, nothing needs to be secured. You aren't pushing the "Bad" away or pulling the "Good" closer. You have stopped being a "Fixer" (Chapter 8) and started being a **Witness.**

The world does not change when you drop your labels. Birth continues. Decay continues. The geopolitical fighting you saw in Chapter 9 continues. The stars move as they always have.

But your **Relationship** to it has become still.

There is nothing to defend because there is nothing separate enough to require defense. You are the mountain, you are the weather, and you are the valley all at once. This is the ultimate "No-Label" truth: You aren't a person in a world; you are the world experiencing itself through a person.

This is the quiet, unshakable peace. Not the peace of a "Good Deal," but the peace of **Sovereignty.** You see the continuous unfolding of life without interference. You see the crickets, the awards, the empty room, and the Middle Eastern woman, and you don't call them "Tragedies" or "Triumphs." You call them **Present.**

You have returned to the "Original Code." The interference has stopped. The "God-Bias" is silent. And in that silence, for the first time, you are truly, undeniably, and perfectly **Restored.**

"The world was never broken; it was only your lens that was shattered. To have a World Restored is to finally stop looking for a 'Meaning' and to start observing the 'Is.' The silence is no longer a void—it is the source."

Epilogue: The Guest in the Infinite

I have spent my life watching the world tremble. I have seen men and women tear each other apart over egos built on shadows and false beliefs. I have seen them cower before things that do not exist in the physical world, but only in the ink of ancient pages.

Because I wanted to understand the source of this trembling, I read them all. I sat with the **Quran,** the **Bible**, and the **Gita**. I walked through the corridors of the world's major scriptures, and what I found at the center of nearly every temple was a dual-headed monster: **The Fear to Live and the Fear to Die.**

Fear thy God. Fear His wrath. Fear the afterlife.

We have been sold a version of the Divine that functions like a celestial debt collector. But let us apply the **Clinical Eye** (Chapter 6) to this concept. I am not saying God does not exist; look at the complexity of a single cell or the rotation of a galaxy—there is undeniably a Source, a Creator, an Original Code.

But look at our position. We are the apex of the food chain, the most complex biological systems on this planet. Why would a Creator capable of weaving the laws of physics require the cowering fear of His own creation? A father does not want his children to live in terror of his belt; he wants them to walk with the grace of their own potential. The "God-Bias" (Chapter 5) is not a divine truth; it is a human tool used to keep the "Herd" (Chapter 9) in line.

In our pursuit of greed, fear, and religious validation, we have committed the ultimate crime: we have forgotten our **Natural Calling.** We have become so obsessed with the "Labels" of being a "Success" or a "Pious Follower" that we have muffled the unique frequency we were born to emit.

We try to make ourselves "Larger than Life." We want our names on buildings, our faces on screens, and our 23 awards on the mantle. We want to be "Something." But let us look at the **Cosmic Math** of who we actually are.

I am a man born in a small part of Mumbai. Mumbai is a speck in the state of Maharashtra. Maharashtra is a fraction of India. India is one piece of the Asian continent. Asia is a segment of Earth. Earth is a pebble in the Solar System. The Solar System is one of billions in a single galaxy.

The galaxy is one of trillions in the observable universe.

So, who am I? Through the Clinical Eye, I am **nothing.** You are nothing. We are a microscopic flash of awareness in an infinite dark.

This is not a depressing thought. It is the most liberating realization a human can have. If you are "Nothing," then the weight of being "Perfect" is gone. If you are "Nothing," then the "God-Bias" has no one to punish. If you are "Nothing," the "Fear of Failure" (Chapter 3) has no target to hit.

We are guests in this world. We arrived without an invitation, and we will leave without a choice. We do not know if our duration is eighty years or eighty minutes.

When you realize you are a guest, your relationship to "Greed" and "Fear" changes. They are no longer your enemies; they are simply the "Weather" of the biological system. You don't try to kill your fear—you learn to control the rudder while the wind blows.

The goal of this book was to show you how to stop seeing the world through the distortion of labels. When you remove the "Pious" label, the "Successful" label, and the "Failure" label, what is left is your **Natural Calling.** This is the gift you were born with, the "Original Code" that was suppressed by the kitchen-shouting and the scripture-reading of your youth.

Find that calling. Use the techniques of the **Clinical Eye** and the **Daily Debridement** to scrape away the social rust until the metal shines again.

People spend their lives wishing for more time because they haven't spent their seconds correctly. They cry at funerals because they lived through a "Temporal Stutter" (Chapter 4), never truly being present for the meal or the conversation.

Make every second count. Not by "Hustling" or "Grinding," but by **Being.**

When you believe in the "Nothingness" of your ego and the "Allness" of your Natural Calling, you become capable of creating unbelievable things. You will write the music, build the life, and share the love that you never imagined possible—not because you are trying to be

"Great," but because you have stopped trying to be anything other than what you are.

The labels are gone. The interference has stopped. The "God-Bias" has been replaced by the "Unblinking Mirror."

Walk out of your door today and look at the trees, the traffic, and the strangers. Don't name them. Don't judge them. Just see them. And in that seeing, you will realize that the "World Restored" (Chapter 10) was never outside of you. It was waiting for you to stop labeling it so it could finally speak.

I was just a guy in Mumbai who stopped fighting the labels. Now, I am just a guest who is enjoying the stay.

Follow your calling. Trust the silence. You are already free.

Dedicated to ***Her***,

Who is still muffled by **Fear**,
Driven by the **Greed** *for safety,*
And blinded by the **God**-*Bias of her ancestors.*

May these words act as the blade that clears the lens, until the cage dissolves and your Natural Calling takes flight.

About The Author

Suraaj Parab is a student of the Clinical Eye. After a career defined by the pursuit of external resonance—earning 23 international awards and a voting membership in the **Recording Academy (GRAMMY® Awards)**—he began the process of **Daily Debridement** to find the **Original Code** beneath the noise of success.

As a composer, bassist, and author, Suraaj's work serves as a sanctuary—a "Neutral" space where the Indian classical tradition meets a global, cross-continental soundscape. Based in Mumbai, he creates in Spanish, Arabic, and Marathi, treating music and literature not as products, but as observations of the human condition.

His mastery of the "Unspoken Word" is recognized by world-class innovators:

- **Endorsements:** Nordstrand Audio and NS Design.
- **Collaborations:** Award-winning projects with maestros like Hamid Saeidi (Usavat).
- **Honors:** Global Music Awards; John Lennon Songwriting Contest Finalist.

Having deconstructed the need for "Certainty" and the "God-Bias," Suraaj now offers his work as an invitation to pause, observe the data of existence, and return to the Infinite.

WWW.SURAAJPARAB.IN

www.ingramcontent.com/pod-product-compliance
Lightning Source LLC
Chambersburg PA
CBHW062355160726
48282CB00041B/908
9789358124194